MoDA STYLE GUIDE

FIFTIESTYLE

home decoration and furnishings from the 1950s

LESLEY HOSKINS

Personal photograph, 1958, image copyright MoDA

First edition 2004 ISBN 978-1904750079,
Revised edition 2016 ISBN 978-0-9565340-7-1

Front Cover Images (clockwise left to right):
Ceiling lamps designed by Bernard Stern, The Daily Mail Ideal Home Book, 1957, courtesy of Daily Mail / Solo Syndication (BADDA714)
Wallpaper samples, The Architects' Book of One Hundred Wallpapers, WPM, 1956-57, image courtesy of MoDA (SC31B-G)
Kitchen storage area, Daily Mail Book of Bungalow Plans, 1958, courtesy of Daily Mail / Solo Syndication (BADDA 716)
Photograph of a living room, The Curtain Book, about 1955, courtesy of Rufflette (BADDA256)

CONTENTS

Introduction	3
Furniture	5
Curtains, cushions and upholstery	13
Walls and paint	21
Flooring	29
Lighting	35
Finishing touches	41
Kitchens	47
Fireplaces and Heating	53
Bathrooms	59
Further Reading	62

INTRODUCTION

The 1950s was a period of reconstruction and change. Modernity, as a reaction to the social, economic and political conditions of the pre-war period, was an important driving force.

The aftermath of the Second World War (1939-1945) left a desperate need for new housing. Between 1945 and 1957 two and a half million new homes were built, 75 per cent of them by local authorities. These new homes enjoyed a good standard of services and equipment, but they were restricted in space. This, alongside a growing informality of family and social life, encouraged the adoption of dual-function rooms, 'through rooms' and even open-plan living. Many of these houses and flats were built in a new, intentionally modern, style. They had flat facades, with large windows, and shallow pitched roofs. Rectangular areas of tile hanging, weatherboarding or rendering added an asymmetrical grid of colour and texture to the brick face.

Modern Homes and Homemaking Illustrated, 1958, © www.timeincukcontent.com

Front cover of Practical Householder, October 1957,
© www.timeincukcontent.com

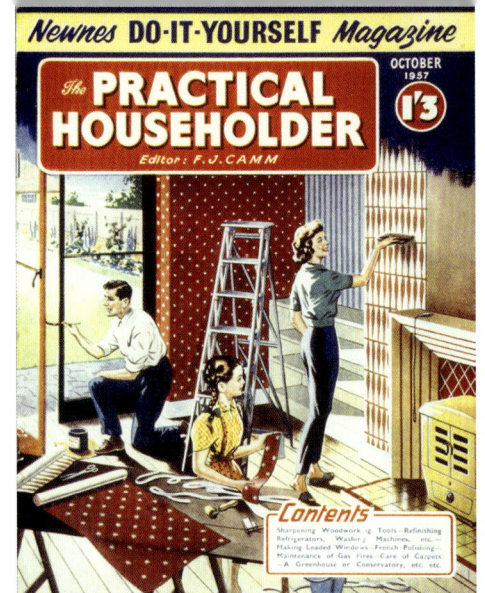

The 1950s saw a frenzy of interest in home making as people returned to domestic life after the disruptions of the war. The increasing availability of goods, the development of DIY products and a rise in incomes, meant that consumers had time and money to spend on decoration and furnishing.

Young people particularly were keen that this decoration and furnishing should be modern. They were encouraged by a flurry of exhibitions (most notably the Festival of Britain in 1951), institutions (such as the Council of Industrial Design, which was established in 1944) and publications (like *House & Garden*), which all promoted a vision of 'good design'. The 'good design' movement, influenced by modernist ideals, endorsed well-made functional goods and the honest use of materials, especially wood. It could support both the spiky and colourful 'contemporary' style as well the more sober 'Scandinavian'.

For a while popular taste and 'good design' coincided but, as incomes continued to rise, and as more and more products came on to the market, the consensus of the early part of the decade gave way to diversity.

FURNITURE

With less space and an increasingly informal attitude to the living areas of the home, furniture layouts were changing. Many new homes no longer had a separate dining room. Instead there was either a living-dining room or a kitchen-dining room. The combined use of this single space made it convenient to have furniture that could be easily moved. The large, solid, three-piece living-room suites and substantial dining-room furniture of the interwar period gave way to lighter pieces. Many easy chairs and settees of the 1950s had wooden legs rather than solid bases. There was also less differentiation in style between living-room and dining-room furniture, as they now often inhabited the same space. However, it was conventional to keep the eating area notionally separate. In a kitchen-diner there was sometimes a counter dividing the cooking from the eating. In a living-dining room, a sideboard or a room divider (a new type of furniture, designed exactly for this purpose) placed at right angles to the wall could create a distinct dining space. Increasing TV ownership during the decade also had an impact. This new item competed with the fireplace as the focal point of the living room.

As ever, furniture was available in a variety of styles and qualities. Initially, many people continued to favour items that were hardly distinguishable from those of the 1930s – solid suites and stained oak. There was also a vogue for the Regency and Victorian revivals. However, the most clearly recognisable idiom of the period, showcased to great effect at the 1951 Festival of Britain, was the 'contemporary', with its tapering, splayed legs. The Scandinavian style was also popular; it was similar to the 'contemporary', but with squarer, sleeker lines. Both emphasised the surface and texture of the wooden elements - oak at first, teak and other exotic woods later.

ILLUSTRATION 1 & 2
Colour and Pattern in the Home, Noel Carrington, 1954, reproduced with kind permission of B.T. Batsford, part of Pavilion Books

ILLUSTRATION 1 & 2 The Design and Industries Association (DIA), which promoted what it regarded as good modern design, exhibited these two room sets at Charing Cross station in 1953. Visitors were asked to 'Register Your Choice'. The room on the top left, with its solid suite, dark oak furniture, mottled wallpaper and beige tiled fireplace, represents a conservative taste little different from that of the 1930s.

The room on the bottom left has all the features of what the DIA considered exemplary modern design. The wingback easy chairs and settee evoke traditional English forms but their pale wooden legs and arms suggest lightness and flexibility as well as taking up little space. The sideboard is arranged to separate the sitting area from the dining area of the dual-purpose room. The knee-high, rectangular, splay-legged coffee table is a characteristic item of the period. Fifty-eight per cent of visitors preferred this room.

ILLUSTRATION 3
The Happy Home, Good Housekeeping Institute, about 1950

ILLUSTRATION 3 Late eighteenth and early nineteenth century styles, which had been a minority fashion before the war, became more widespread in the 1950s. This Regency-style dining room, with its highly polished wood, implies more formality than the 'contemporary'.

ILLUSTRATION 4
Design in the Festival, The Council of Industrial Design, 1951, image courtesy of MoDA

ILLUSTRATION 5
Catalogue for G-Plan furniture, 1958, courtesy of G Plan Upholstery Ltd

ILLUSTRATION 4 In 1950 only 350,000 households had a TV; by 1960 this had risen to almost ten million. So, should the furniture be oriented around the fireplace or the television? The settee in this room-set at the Festival of Britain turns its back on the TV but the two armchairs can be easily shifted as required.

ILLUSTRATION 5 The G-Plan range, made by Gomme of High Wycombe, was launched in 1953. Initially it was made of oak but later output, influenced by the Scandinavian style, was often of teak. G-Plan advertised widely, emphasising the versatility and flexibility of its system, which allowed people to buy individual items as needed rather than complete suites.

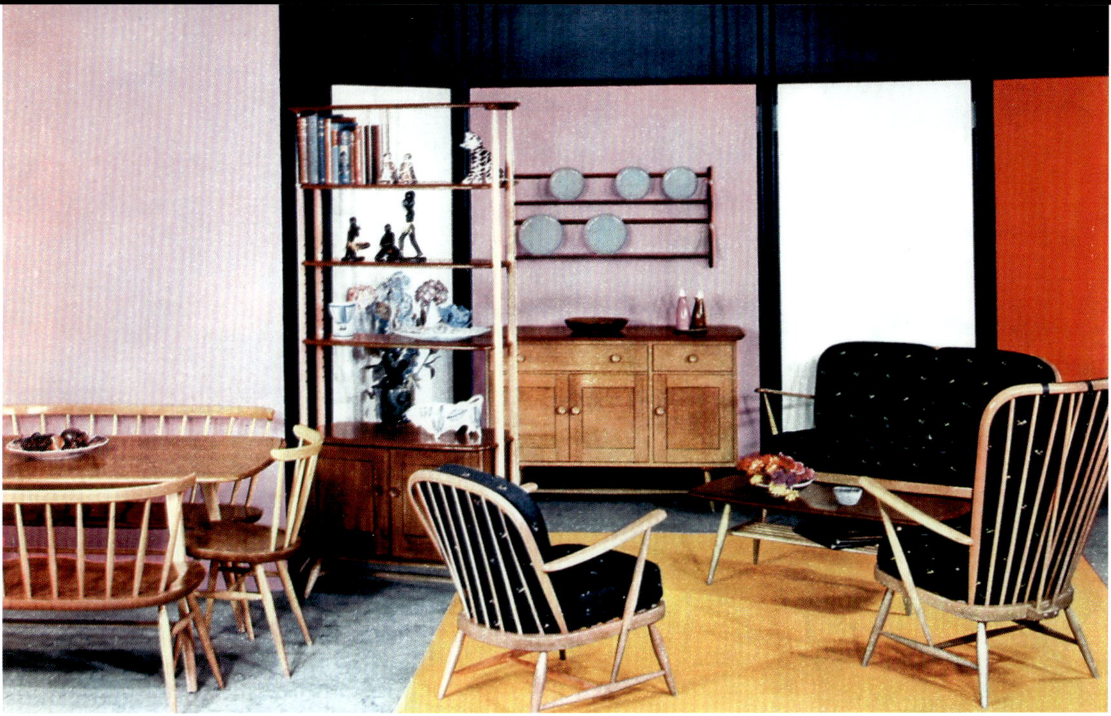

ILLUSTRATION 6
Catalogue for Ercol furniture, about 1955, courtesy of Ercol Furniture Ltd

ILLUSTRATION 7
Catalogue for Greaves & Thomas furniture, late 1950s

ILLUSTRATION 6 Ercol was another well-known brand. Their products were contemporary versions of traditional English Windsor chairs, made up-to-date by the use of light oak, splayed legs and upward-sweeping arms.

ILLUSTRATION 7 Convertible couches, which opened out to provide a spare bed, were a popular option for people with limited space. The Put-U-Up range by Greaves & Thomas was solidly made and its 'contemporary' styling appealed to young couples with modern tastes.

ILLUSTRATION 8 & 9
Personal photographs, 1958, images copyright MoDA

ILLUSTRATION 8 & 9 These two photographs show the living-dining room of a new house in north London in the late 1950s, taken just after the young owners had moved in. The furnishing is not quite complete - there are no curtains or a rug - but the inhabitants wanted an uncluttered modern look.

The couch is a Greaves & Thomas Put-U-Up. It features the upright back and legs that were starting to take over from the angled and splayed styling of the early part of the decade. Poodles, often sporting an elaborate 'lion cut', were all the rage in the 1950s.

Although the Kandya dining table and chairs look very spindly they were substantial enough to be in use fifty years later.

ILLUSTRATION 10
Catalogue for Berry Furniture, late 1950s

ILLUSTRATION 11
Catalogue for Danish Royal Systems furniture, late 1950s, courtesy of dk3

ILLUSTRATION 10 A number of techniques and materials developed for use during the Second World War were subsequently adapted for the manufacture of consumer goods. This dining-room suite in the 'contemporary' style makes use of melamine – easy to clean, colourful and inexpensive.

ILLUSTRATION 11 The room divider - a combination of sideboard or cupboard with open shelves above - was a key item of 1950s furniture. It was used to make a notional break between the different areas of a multi-purpose room without taking up too much space or blocking the light. It could also be placed against a wall, where it gave a much lighter effect than the traditional, more solid, china cabinet.

This example is made of teak and was suitable for a living-dining room. There were similar dividers for the kitchen-dining room, though the finish would more usually have been a plastic veneer.

ILLUSTRATION 12
Daily Mail Book of Bungalow Plans, 1958, courtesy of Daily Mail / Solo Syndication

ILLUSTRATION 12 The new-found need for flexibility did not affect sleeping areas to the same extent as living spaces. Although there was a growing notion that children's rooms should be furnished to allow use for homework and hobbies, this only began to have a major impact late in the decade, when increased affluence allowed the purchase of additional heating.

A survey of the early 1950s found that young couples setting up home for the first time put the highest priority on furnishing their bedroom and that they spent more on it than the living room. A master bedroom was often furnished with a substantial suite, including bed, wardrobe, dressing table and stool.

CURTAINS AND UPHOLSTERY

The 1950s was a great time for the design of printed textiles. After the drab colours and shortages during and after World War Two, manufacturers now offered an eager public new, bright, modern fabrics that deliberately avoided traditional or historical references. Printed textiles initially made use of the 'contemporary' idiom, characterised by spiky or cursive lines, abstract shapes and strong colour contrasts. More painterly effects were also available, especially in large-scale floral and scenic designs. Later in the decade these clearly defined motifs gave way to a more all-over, blurry look without losing strength of pattern or colour.

Such designs appealed particularly to the younger consumer. They were at first rather expensive and were sold by shops like Heal's in London, whose range included fabrics by the influential freelance designer Lucienne Day. Her work was amongst that featured at the Festival of Britain and won many awards. But similar patterns soon entered the wider market. David Whitehead Fabrics was especially important in this respect. This company used cheaper textiles (such as spun rayon) and printed by machine rather than by hand, to offer 'contemporary' patterns by named designers at a reasonable price.

As curtains, these striking fabrics suited the large picture windows that were a feature of the time. They hung straight to the bottom of the window or to the floor, usually without a valance or pelmet. To maintain their dramatic impact the adjoining wall was either plain or quietly patterned.

By contrast, upholstery was relatively undecorated and almost always of a woven fabric. Small-scale, discreet patterns were much used, as were plain tweedy or bouclé-like textural effects.

At the same time, more traditional floral prints remained as popular as ever. Printed loose covers were a feature of some less consciously modern schemes, but many used the widespread convention of pairing printed curtains with plainer woven upholstery.

ILLUSTRATION 1
Decorative Art, 1952 – 1953, courtesy of David Whitehead and Sons Ltd

ILLUSTRATION 1 David Whitehead Fabrics ran a glamorous and colourful advertising campaign for their modern designs. This one clearly promotes the use of woven fabrics for upholstery and prints for curtains.

ILLUSTRATION 2 The plain scarlet woven upholstery on the wing chair and the strongly coloured plain walls complement the dramatic effect of the 'contemporary' pattern at the picture window.

ILLUSTRATION 2
The Curtain Book, about 1955, courtesy of Rufflette

ILLUSTRATION 3
Catalogue for Minty furniture, 1959

ILLUSTRATION 3 It was fashionable to use contrasting colours on a single chair. Dark grey and cherry red was a particularly prevalent combination.

CURTAINS AND UPHOLSTERY

ILLUSTRATION 4
Curtain, about 1953, image courtesy of MoDA

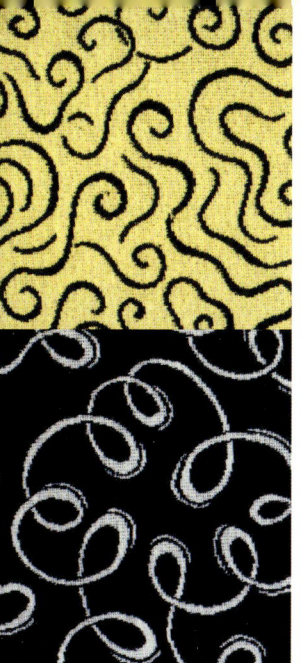

ILLUSTRATION 4 This curtain fabric, designed by Jacqueline Groag, was bought from Heal's. The delicate black lines and abstract shapes are typical of many 'contemporary' patterns.

ILLUSTRATION 5 The colouring of these upholstery fabrics is typical of 'contemporary' patterns of the earlier years of the 1950s.

ILLUSTRATION 6 This good quality cotton/wool woven textile is in a traditional style, not dissimilar to patterns of the 1930s. Such designs were still very popular in the early fifties and continued in use throughout the decade and beyond.

ILLUSTRATION 5
Woven textiles, about 1955, image courtesy of MoDA

ILLUSTRATION 6
Woven textile, about 1950, image courtesy of MoDA

ILLUSTRATION 7
Printed textile, 1957, image courtesy of MoDA

ILLUSTRATION 7 A traditional floral pattern, with up-dated colouring and treatment. Such a print would have been used mostly for curtains; loose covers were not very fashionable at this time.

ILLUSTRATION 8 Textiles in the bedroom followed similar rules to those in the living areas, though the colours were often in the pink and blue part of the spectrum. Candlewick bedspreads were widely used.

ILLUSTRATION 9 Designs from the later 1950s remained large and colourful but tended to have overall patterns with less clearly delineated individual motifs.

ILLUSTRATION 8
House and Garden, May 1958

ILLUSTRATION 9
*Curtain, about 1960,
image courtesy of MoDA*

ILLUSTRATION 10
House and Garden, July 1958, courtesy of Luxaflex ®

ILLUSTRATION 10 Although large picture windows were fashionable they did not give the privacy that many people found necessary. Nets were a possible way of dealing with this. Venetian blinds, now made in a new lightweight and relatively easy to clean material, had a similar effect but in a more austere modern-looking way.

WALLS AND PAINT

Wallpaper was subject to post-war shortages until the early 1950s, but once it became fully available it was heavily promoted in style and domestic magazines and became fashionable in all parts of the market. Manufacturers commissioned expensive and adventurous modern patterns from well-known freelance artists, whose names added to the cachet of the product and whose designs influenced the mass market.

The wallpapers that appeared most in the magazines and that now seem to us particularly characteristic of the 1950s were 'contemporary'. They usually featured 'hand-drawn' graphic lines and small abstract or geometric motifs; their colours were bold - yellow, grey, green, black, white, red and mauve. There was also a spate of illustrative papers, some of them with motifs related to food and drink, specially designed for the kitchen or dining room.

'Contemporary' patterns appealed most to the younger consumer, setting up home for the first time after the shortages of the war years. However it took a while for these wallpapers to dominate the market as much as they did the magazines. In 1952 they were only four per cent of output and twenty per cent in 1956. Most early 1950s patterns actually continued in much the same style as in the 1930s – mottled, indistinct, textured 'porridge' patterns in beiges, oranges and greens, trimmed with a narrow paper border. Also popular, especially in the upper part of the market, were traditional patterns – Victorian sprigs and Regency stripes and medallions. But by the end of the decade the 'contemporary' had captured the bulk of sales.

Paint showed a similar trajectory, with beiges, greens and browns giving way to much brighter colours. House & Garden magazine popularised a range of strong tones, including the particularly fashionable mustards, olive greens and deep reds. These eye-catching colours were used for walls or exterior doors; interior woodwork was usually white or off-white.

ILLUSTRATION 1
Paper from E. Cole wallpaper pattern book, 1952-53, image courtesy of MoDA

ILLUSTRATION 1 The majority of wallpapers in the early 1950s had indistinct, mottled all-over patterns and were used with a narrow paper border at the level of the picture rail. In this example the pale green leaves are heavily embossed – the sign of an expensive paper. Similar colours had been popular since the early 1930s and continued so well into the mid-1950s.

ILLUSTRATION 2
Paint chart, 1950

ILLUSTRATION 3
Daily Mail Ideal Home Book, 1950-51, courtesy of Sanderson

ILLUSTRATION 2 Paint colours of the early 1950s were also similar to those of the 1930s, when creams, browns and greens predominated. Gloss finishes and stronger colours were mainly for exterior use; cream window frames would be combined with a dark colour for the doors and window bars. Inside, creams and perhaps browns would be used on woodwork. Distemper or flat oil paint (similar to today's eggshell) was used for walls.

ILLUSTRATION 3 Floral patterns and pale, pretty colours were considered particularly suitable for bedrooms. This Sanderson advert for a rosebud sprig paper shows a Victorian revival room scheme.

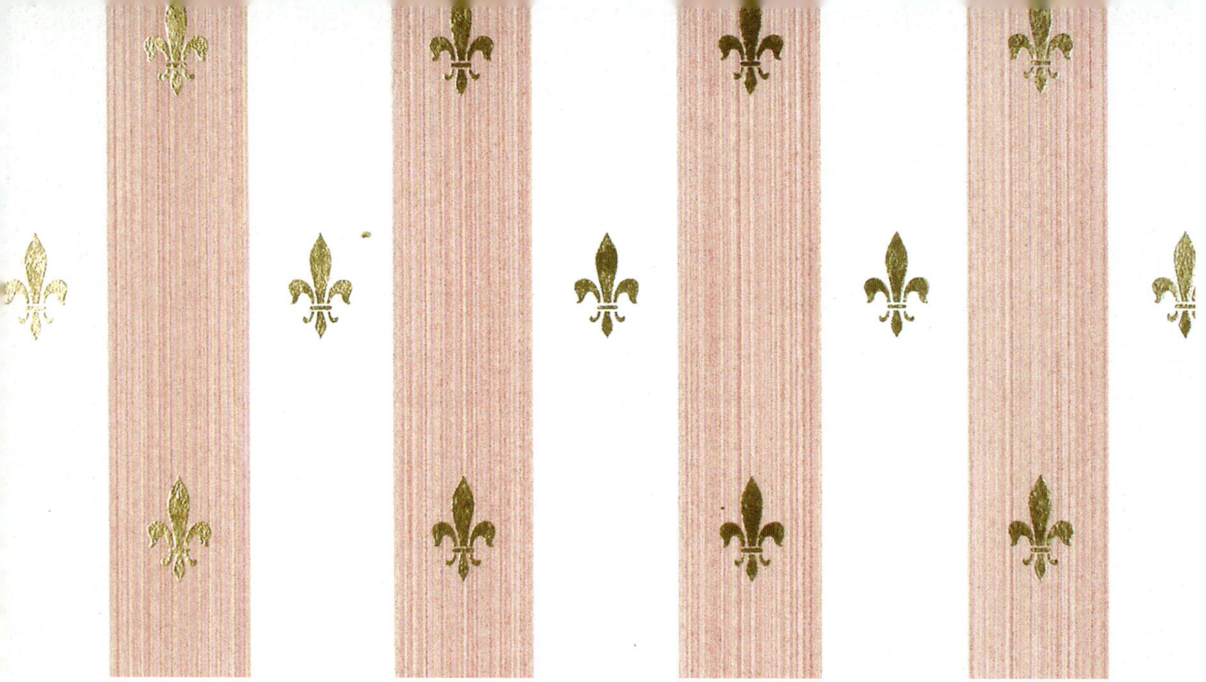

SC53A

ILLUSTRATION 4

Wallpaper from John Line & Sons pattern book, about 1950, image courtesy of MoDA

ILLUSTRATION 5

The Architects' Book of One Hundred Wallpapers, WPM, 1956-57, image courtesy of MoDA

SC31B-G

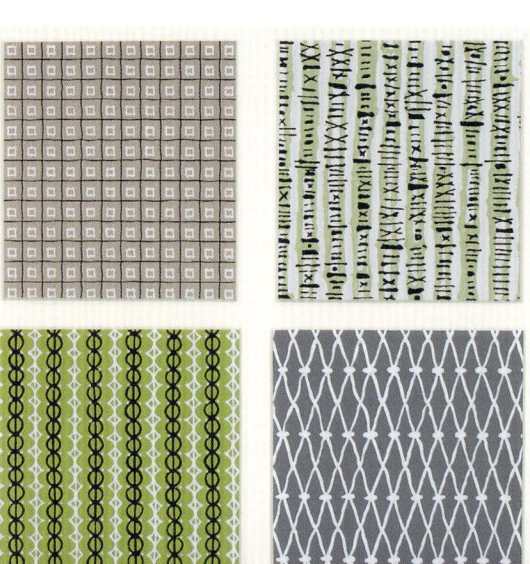

ILLUSTRATION 6
Wallpapers and illustration from Interiors for the Contemporary Home by Cleaver, 1956-57

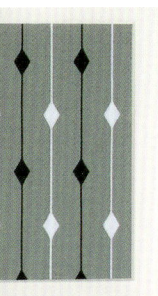

ILLUSTRATION 4 The Regency revival style was fashionable at the upper end of the market. This hand-printed stripe was extremely expensive at 39 shillings a roll (equivalent of approximately £45 today).

ILLUSTRATION 5 Mustard yellow and grey were popular 'contemporary' colours and, in wallpapers, the pattern was often printed in white or black. Although these small-scale abstract patterns are actually printed by machine, the lines are deliberately given a hand-drawn look.

ILLUSTRATION 6 The patterns and colours of some modern papers were too dominant for use all the way round a room. They were intended for a limited area, usually one wall, a chimney breast, or the alcoves, while the rest of the room was papered in a quieter 'companion paper'. This example, manufactured by Crown, was a best seller.

SC60

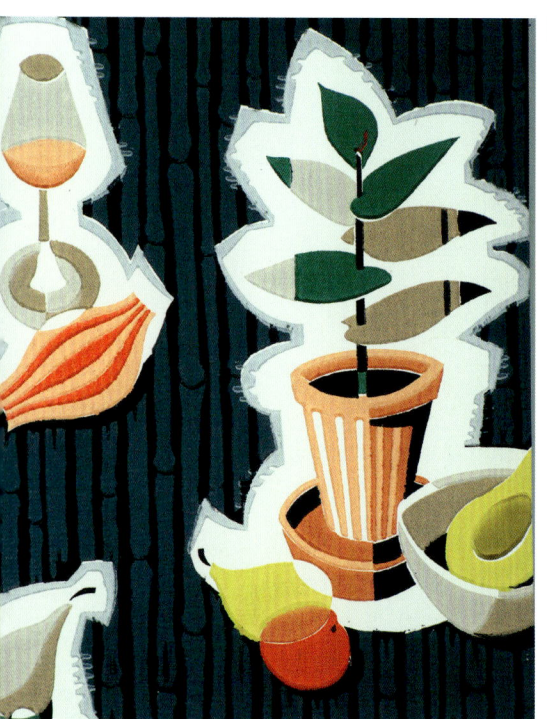

ILLUSTRATION 7

'Wallpaper from Shand Kydd pattern book, 1958-59, image courtesy of MoDA

ILLUSTRATION 8

'Bistro' wallpaper from WPM's Palladio pattern book, 1955, image courtesy of MoDA

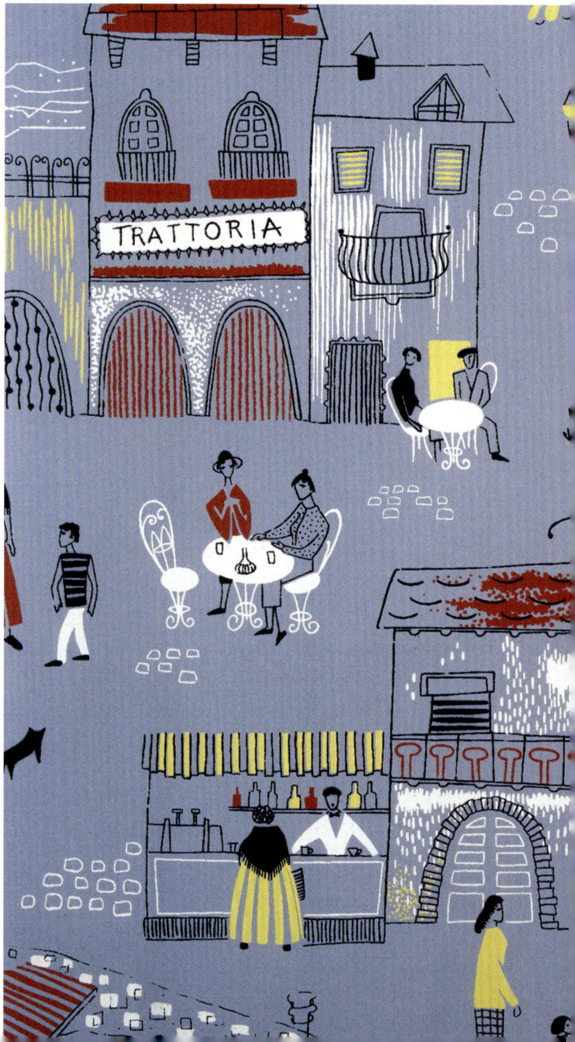

ILLUSTRATION 9
Paint chart for House & Garden colours, 1958

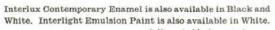

ILLUSTRATION 7 Cheerful patterns with food- and drink-related motifs came on to the market for use in kitchens and dining areas. This example features avocados and glasses of wine – both of which were new and exotic luxuries for the majority of consumers.

ILLUSTRATION 8 With increasing affluence and the development of air travel, more people were now able to take foreign holidays, a fact perhaps reflected in the flurry of wallpapers showing scenes of French and Italian street and café life. Large-scale versions decorated restaurants and coffee bars. Smaller versions were used in the home, especially in dining areas.

ILLUSTRATION 9 Domestic magazines actively promoted modern designs and colours. *House & Garden* even endorsed a range of its own colours, which changed yearly.

The really strong colours were intended for exterior use, especially front doors. Inside, as with wallpaper, one wall might be strongly coloured but the rest of the room would be quieter. Woodwork was usually white or off-white.

Gloss was used for woodwork and emulsion or distemper for walls.

WALLS AND PAINT

ILLUSTRATION 10
'Cut Out' wallpaper, designed by Terence Conran for Crown's Modus range 1960, image courtesy of MoDA

ILLUSTRATION 10 By the end of the decade linear, 'hand-drawn' motifs were beginning to give way to patterns with larger areas of flat colour, as in this expensive 'designer' paper.

FLOORING

Carpet continued to be an expensive item but two important factors contributed to its growing use during the 1950s. One was the general increase in incomes towards the end of the decade and the other was the development of a new, cheaper type. Tufted carpets, introduced from 1953 by companies such as Cyril Lord and Kossett, were considerably more affordable than traditionally woven Axminsters and Wiltons, partly because of a fast new production technique and partly because they were generally made of man-made or synthetic fibres rather than wool.

There were a range of designs on offer - traditional oriental or floral patterns, 'contemporary' designs with graphic patterns similar to those on wallpapers and textiles, and plain colours. Axminsters and Wiltons could be had in all these styles but tufted carpets were mostly only available in plain or tweedy finishes. Plain carpet suited the modern approach to furnishing, which confined pattern to walls and curtains. The problem of keeping a plain carpet looking clean was alleviated by the growing ownership of vacuum cleaners (seventy-two per cent of households by 1963). It was also increasingly popular to have fitted carpets and, again, vacuums played a part in supporting this fashion.

Many people could not afford much, or even any, carpet. If they had only a limited budget, they would prioritise a carpet for the living room. Lino or thermoplastic or vinyl tiles were a cheaper finish. They were used throughout the home, with or without rugs or carpet squares. But they were a particularly popular choice for hallways, landings, bedrooms and, of course, kitchens where new colourful patterns helped to make a bright and cheerful working environment for the housewife.

At the consciously modern end of the market there was a fashion for uncarpeted plain floors in finishes such as wood block, cork tiles, lino or rubber.

ILLUSTRATION 1
'Homes and Gardens, October 1958

ILLUSTRATION 1 Completely plain, wall-to-wall wool carpets were both expensive to buy and difficult to keep clean. Nevertheless, they were a smart and fashionable choice for those who could afford them. A similar effect could be achieved by buying a tufted carpet in a man-made or synthetic fibre.

ILLUSTRATION 2 Traditional carpet patterns remained extremely popular. The design of this wool Axminster could almost have been drawn in the late nineteenth century.

ILLUSTRATION 3 Consumers preferred traditionally made wool carpets if they could afford them. This carpet is fitted throughout the living-dining room but it was alternatively available in strips or squares. The 'contemporary' pattern was called Skaters' Trails.

CAMBRIA
wall-to-wall carpet
seamless up to 12 ft. wide

MJC/72/328

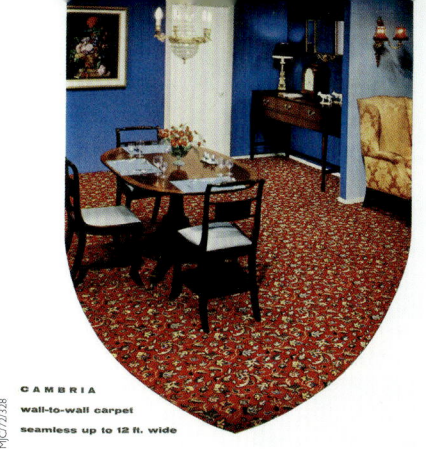

ILLUSTRATION 2

Homes and Gardens, October 1958

ILLUSTRATION 3

Homes and Gardens, October 1958

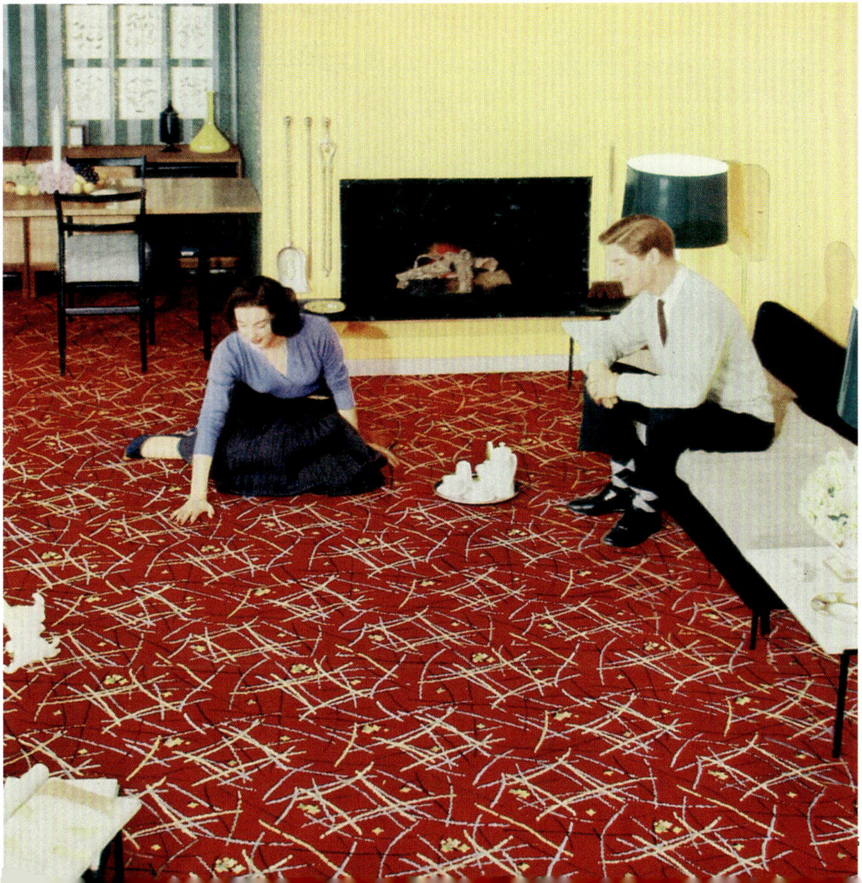

MJC/72/328

ILLUSTRATION 4
Daily Mail Book of Bungalow Plans, 1958, courtesy of Daily Mail / Solo Syndication

ILLUSTRATION 4 Lino was a very popular finish for kitchen floors. It usually had a mottled pattern, which did not show the dirt as much as a completely plain surface. New, bright patterns, like this, helped to make the kitchen a cheerful place.

ILLUSTRATION 5 Marley offered both vinyl and, as here, thermoplastic tiles in a wide range of colours. This advertisement shows a living room without any rug or carpet.

ILLUSTRATION 5
Homes and Gardens, June 1956, courtesy of Tarkett Ltd

ILLUSTRATION 6
Daily Mail Ideal Home Book, 1957, courtesy of Daily Mail / Solo Syndication

ILLUSTRATION 6 This ultra-modern room has cork tile flooring. This, and alternatives such as rubber tiles and hardwood block or strip, particularly appealed to people with a fashionable modern taste for lack of clutter and natural finishes. Many new homes were built with such flooring but it could also be used to up-date older accommodation.

ILLUSTRATION 7
Homes and Gardens, February 1959, © www.timeincukcontent.com

ILLUSTRATION 7 In many new houses of the later 1950s, large glass doors led directly onto a small patio or terrace, 'bringing the garden into the house'. This was an intermediate area, ideally treated as an outside room. It needed a floor finish that was weatherproof and easy to clean but also suitable for furniture. This picture shows a loggia with coloured concrete paving.

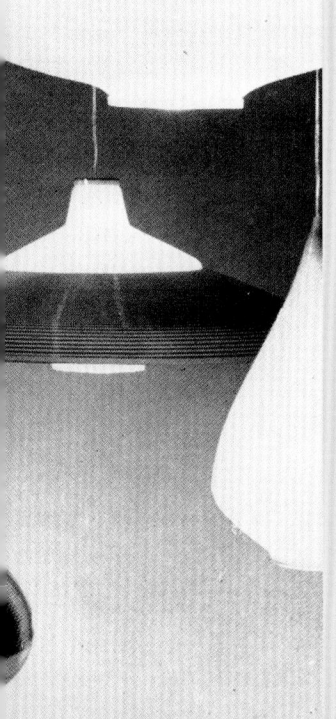

LIGHTING

By 1951 almost ninety per cent of all homes were wired for electricity, which was now accepted as the power for lighting. However, the number and type of lights in a single household could vary considerably, depending largely on the degree of affluence. It was nonetheless generally true that people had fewer wall sockets than we regard as normal today. However, as incomes rose during the 1950s, lighting became more complex.

It was standard to have a central ceiling fitting in each room giving general illumination. But people were advised to have additional provision, both to create a more interesting and pleasing effect but also to support special activities. Wired-in wall fittings gave attractive pools of brightness. Standard, desk and table lamps provided direct light for things like reading, sewing, and homework in living rooms and bedrooms. There was a fashion for pull-down overhead lights above the dining table. Bathrooms needed illumination for the mirror and sink. There was some discussion about the best equipment for the kitchen; fluorescent tubes were a possibility, though not frequently used in a domestic situation at this time; much more common were central ceiling fittings with opalescent globe shades, which gave a very general diffused light.

There was a huge variety of lamps and shades on offer. Coloured opalescent glass bowls, chandeliers with candlestick or glass-cup fittings, and lanterns for the hall had changed little since before the war. At the consciously modern end of the spectrum were the 'contemporary' effects with their spindly black or metallic legs. These often featured large drum, funnel or 'Chinese hat' shades, made of pleated or rimpled paper, plastic or fabric. Spun aluminium was also used, sometimes in the fashionable bright and cheerful colours. Large globe or tear-drop lanterns of paper, milky glass or one of the new man-made materials, such as cellulose, went particularly well with the Scandinavian style of the time.

ILLUSTRATION 1
Ideal Home, November 1955, photographer: Stanley Chapman,
© *www.timeincukcontent.com*

ILLUSTRATION 2
The Book of Good Housekeeping, about 1955
Private collection

ILLUSTRATION 1 This is the living room of a young architect's home. It is extremely well provided with subsidiary lighting. The pottery table lamp on the shelf in the alcove to the left of the fire has a fabric drum shade. The floor standard lamp and the wall light on a swivel arm are both typical of the contemporary style – they have very slender legs and pleated 'Chinese hat' shades.

ILLUSTRATION 2 A selection of colourful shades in the modern idiom. They include pleated paper, straw matting, milky glass and spun aluminium in the fashionable drum, 'Chinese hat', funnel and tear-drop globe shapes.

LIGHTING 37

ILLUSTRATION 3
The Good Housekeeping Book of Home Decorating, 1947

ILLUSTRATION 4
*Colour and Pattern in the Home, Noel Carrington, 1954,
reproduced with kind permission of B.T. Batsford, part of Pavilion Books Company Limited*

ILLUSTRATION 3 Some people made their own lamp bases from vases, jars and bottles. These shades are home-made too; the shop-bought frames are covered with wallpaper, muslin, parchment and silk.

ILLUSTRATION 4 Pierced metal funnel shades, either brightly coloured, as here, or in unpainted spun aluminium were often promoted as good modern design by magazines and decorating advice books.

ILLUSTRATION 5 These drop globes by Rotaflex were made from spun cellulose acetate. Like the equally fashionable Japanese-inspired paper shades, they gave a diffused general light and shielded the eyes from the glare of the naked bulb.

ILLUSTRATION 5
Ceiling lamps designed by Bernard Stern, The Daily Mail Ideal Home Book, 1957, courtesy of Daily Mail / Solo Syndication

ILLUSTRATION 6
The Daily Mail Ideal Home Book 1952-53, courtesy of Daily Mail / Solo Syndication

ILLUSTRATION 7
Catalogue for the Houndsditch Warehouse Company, 1950s

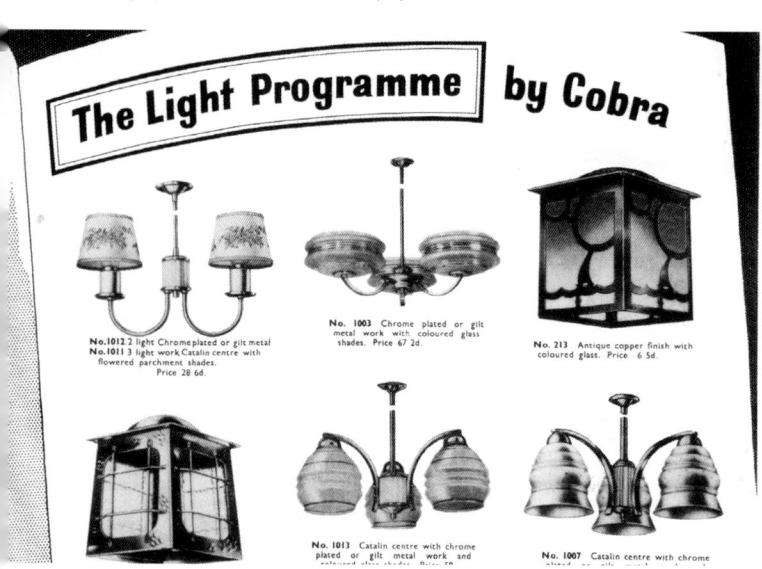

ILLUSTRATION 6 When raised to ceiling level this shade gave an overall general light. When pulled down over the table it gave a more intimate effect.

ILLUSTRATION 7 Lights like these had changed little since before the war. They were just as popular as those in the 'contemporary' style.

FINISHING TOUCHES

Two conflicting trends affected the number of decorative objects in people's homes in the 1950s. On the one hand, as the decade progressed, consumers had more money to spend on this kind of thing; on the other hand, widely held modernist ideals promoted the reduction of unnecessary bric-a-brac. Photographs of homes of the time indicate that, for most people, affluence was the stronger influence; decorative objects were displayed on mantelpieces, shelves, window ledges, room dividers and wall units. Many of these ornaments would have been gifts, souvenirs and hand-me-downs, kept for reasons of sentiment as much as of style or fashion. But new items were also available in the whole range of 1950s styles – traditional, 'contemporary' and the more austere modernist or Scandinavian.

Scandinavian design was much promoted and appealed to the design conscious consumer. A great deal of glass, pottery and metal-ware was imported, while domestic production often showed its influence. A related element of fashionable taste was for the 'hand-made' – or at least for things that looked hand-made. 'Studio' (hand-thrown or hand-painted) pottery, coarsely woven fabrics and hand-blown glass were all popular.

The more cheerful 'contemporary' or 'Festival of Britain' style also made its mark on ornaments and decorative items. Tableware, for example, often featured spikily drawn motifs and the trademark use of black.

In all the consciously modern styles, there was a tendency towards rounded, organic shapes which could be seen across a wide range of items such as ceramics, glassware and cutlery.

The use of houseplants, especially tradescantia and cacti, was very characteristic of the period. They were usually seen on window ledges or shelves, in individual pots with decorative wire holders. Suitable varieties could be trained up the wall.

Pictures were most often displayed on the fireplace wall. It was fashionable to have just one or two, hung asymmetrically.

ILLUSTRATION 1
*Daily Mail Ideal Home Book 1956,
courtesy of Daily Mail / Solo Syndication*

ILLUSTRATION 1 Houseplants are a key decorative feature in the living room of this modern terraced house in Hatfield New Town. The fireplace forms the focus of the room, with ornaments on the mantelpiece and the chimney wall highlighted by a picture and a trailing plant. Asymmetry, as seen in the arrangement on the wall and in the shapes of many modern objects, was a feature of the period.

ILLUSTRATION 3
*Furnishing the Small Home,
Margaret Merivale, 1953*

ILLUSTRATION 2
*Decorative Art: The Studio Yearbook of Furnishing &
Decoration, 1952-53*

ILLUSTRATION 2 Sweden and Finland had flourishing glass industries and exported a great deal into Britain at this time. Swedish vases were very often pear-shaped. Made of heavy, hand-blown plain glass, either colourless or grey or dark blue, they had a craft quality that was much admired.

ILLUSTRATION 3 Studio-type pottery, either actually hand-made or looking hand-made, was fashionable. These examples are from Sweden. In Britain both Poole and Rye made similar items, characterised by gourd shapes and hand-painted banding and dots.

FINISHING TOUCHES

ILLUSTRATION 4
Daily Mail Ideal Home Book 1957,
courtesy of Daily Mail / Solo Syndication

ILLUSTRATION 4 1950s 'good design' celebrated natural materials. So, even for formal meals, it was considered preferable to dispense with 'old-fashioned' tablecloths leaving the wooden table visible. Individual placemats were used instead. In this illustration they are of rough-woven Irish linen, as are the napkins. The glassware is undecorated, in keeping with the modernist aesthetic.

ILLUSTRATION 5 The use of smooth rounded forms can be seen in this cutlery designed by David Mellor. The curved blade was a departure from the traditional straight-edged knife.

ILLUSTRATION 5
Daily Mail Ideal Home Book, 1957,
courtesy of Daily Mail / Solo Syndication

44 FINISHING TOUCHES

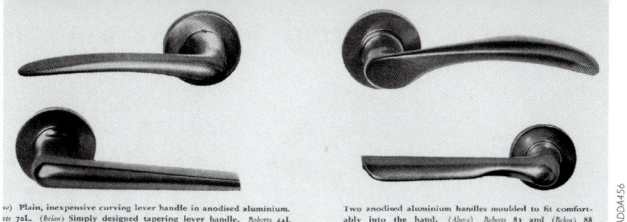

ILLUSTRATION 6
Daily Mail Ideal Home Book, 1956, courtesy of Daily Mail / Solo Syndication

ILLUSTRATION 6 Similar shapes can be seen in these moulded anodized aluminium door handles. It was suggested that bar handles were more appropriate to the flush doors of new houses than door knobs. They were also considered to be more functional – you could open the door with your elbow if your hands were full.

ILLUSTRATION 7 Mass-produced tableware with the Homemaker pattern, designed by Enid Seeney, was sold through Woolworths from 1958. Its motifs celebrate 'contemporary' design and the home. It was an extremely popular range. Other companies, such as Midwinter, also made tableware with 'contemporary' patterns and with curving profiles and outlines reminiscent of the shape of a TV screen.

ILLUSTRATION 7
Plate, 1958 or afterwards, image courtesy of MoDA

FINISHING TOUCHES

ILLUSTRATION 8
Michael Farr, Design in British Industry, 1955, courtesy of WWRD Group

ILLUSTRATION 8 This English, machine-pressed glass bowl, with its detailed fluting, would never have been seen in the design magazines but was nevertheless a typical and popular item of tableware.

ILLUSTRATION 9 Along with TVs, record players became common household items. Some were large pieces of cabinet furniture but the Dansette, first introduced in 1950-51, was the size of a small suitcase with a handle, making it relatively portable. The 1950s saw the birth of the 'teenager' as a separate consumer group and the Dansette became a teenage icon - in spite of the fact that it could cost about two weeks' wages..

ILLUSTRATION 9
Catalogue for the Houndsditch Warehouse Company, 1950s

KITCHENS

In the 1950s the kitchen changed from being a straightforwardly practical and functional part of the house, arranged and decorated accordingly, to a more integral part of the social space. It became less private, more open to family and social life, and its appearance changed to reflect this.

For all but the very wealthy, live-in servants were a thing of the past and it was fully recognised that the housewife would do the work. This further encouraged the existing trend towards efficient labour-saving layouts, easy-clean surfaces and the integration of labour-saving appliances such as washing machines, refrigerators and electric kettles. Almost all homes now had electricity and many had a good supply of sockets, so the use of appliances became possible for all those that could afford them. As affluence increased throughout the decade, the number of households with such gadgets rose significantly.

In order to meet the targets of the massive post-war home-building programme, the size of new houses and flats was kept relatively small. The amount of circulation and storage space was reduced and there was a trend towards combining what had previously been separate rooms; one such combination was the kitchen-dining room, sometimes with an additional utility room. Although, in actuality, many people already ate most of their family meals in the kitchen, in the 1950s this became an officially recommended practice for new houses built in both the public and private sectors. This meant that visitors as well as the family now entered the kitchen. Since it was also where the housewife was recognised to spend much of her time, the kitchen now had a reason to be attractive as well as functional. Colourful new furnishings, wallpapers and textiles were introduced, signalling that this previously purely functional area was now part of the living space of the home.

ILLUSTRATION 1
Personal photograph, about 1955

ILLUSTRATION 2
Homes and Gardens, June 1953, courtesy of Frigidaire

ILLUSTRATION 1 Most new housing had a gas or electric stove, although many people in older accommodation continued to use solid fuel ranges of one sort or another. This kitchen in a new bungalow built in 1955 was equipped with both. It also has an electric kettle as well as a pair for use on the range.

ILLUSTRATION 2 This refrigerator cost about fifteen times the average weekly wage in 1953. But, as wages grew, so did ownership of appliances and, by the early 1960s, thirty per cent of households had a refrigerator. They could be run on either gas or electricity. They were usually shiny white and incorporated into the work surface. They cut down the need for frequent shopping and for larder space.

ILLUSTRATION 3 Washing machines were rather more prevalent than refrigerators; they were found in forty-five per cent of households by the early 1960s. They too were usually shiny white. They were not plumbed in and had to be pulled up to the sink to be filled with water from a pipe. The user had to take the wet items out and put them through the attached wringer. Although they did cut down on the heavy labour of hand washing, the weekly wash was still a time-consuming and exhausting activity.

HOME LAUNDRY
by Josephine March

Easier ways of washing, drying and ironing are described in this survey of improvements in laundry equipment

The Hoover Mark III washing machine has a detachable automatic wringer with 10-in. rollers. The wringer can be stored away on a cradle inside the machine and

ILLUSTRATION 3
Daily Mail Ideal Home Book, 1956, courtesy of Daily Mail / Solo Syndication

ILLUSTRATION 4 Efficiency and cleanliness was part of the kitchen aesthetic, seen in the unbroken run of worktop and glass-fronted wall cabinets in this illustration of Fleetway units. However, the decorative use of bright colours was in this case more important than whiteness, which was a continuing symbol of hygiene.

ILLUSTRATION 4
Catalogue for Fleetway kitchen cupboards, about 1960

furnish **your** kitchen completely with FLEETWAY

FLEETWAY   FLEETWAY

49

ILLUSTRATION 5
Homes and Gardens, June 1957, courtesy of Formica Group

ILLUSTRATION 5 Formica, an American plastic laminate, was a common feature of the modern 1950s kitchen. Applied to tables, worktops and unit doors it was hard-wearing and easily cleaned, and was available in a wide range of attractive and colourful patterns.

ILLUSTRATION 6 Manufacturers began producing all kinds of kitchen equipment and furnishings in cheerful colours and patterns. Wallpapers and curtaining intended for this part of the house often featured food or cooking motifs.

ILLUSTRATION 6
The Daily Mail Book of Bungalow Plans, 1958

ILLUSTRATION 7
Homes and Gardens, June 1959

ILLUSTRATION 8
The Flat Book by J.L. Martin and S. Speight, 1939
Courtesy of The Shenval Press.

ILLUSTRATION 7 Many plastics, developed originally for industrial use, were exploited for domestic use after the Second World War. This advert states that 'Houseware made from 'Alkathene' will not break, chip or rust. It is light, easy to clean, silent in use and comes in a wide range of gay colours'.

ILLUSTRATION 8 It was possible to make a distinction between the eating and cooking areas of the kitchen-diner by decorating them differently. Here the 'working' part of the room has hard, shiny surfaces while the eating area has the softer finishes of wood, wallpaper and upholstery.

KITCHENS 51

ILLUSTRATION 9
House and Garden, February 1953, courtesy of Denby Pottery

ILLUSTRATION 9 Island units, often with rounded ends, were sometimes introduced to make a division between the kitchen and dining areas. Because food preparation was now visible to the people eating and to cut down on washing up, manufacturers introduced ranges of attractive oven-to-tableware, which did away with the need to use cooking pans as well as serving dishes. Denby ware was especially popular.

ILLUSTRATION 10 Cooking utensil motifs feature on the curtains in this kitchen in the North East towards the end of the decade.

ILLUSTRATION 10
Personal photograph, about 1960, © Beamish, The North of England Open Air Museum

FIREPLACES AND HEATING

Generally speaking, homes got warmer during the 1950s and it became less common to find frost on the inside of the bedroom and bathroom windows on winter mornings.

Most people relied mainly on solid fuel for their heating needs and there was usually a coal fire in the living room. There were some improvements in the performance of open fires but closed stoves were more efficient and, with glass doors, allowed the fire to remain visible. They functioned on coke and anthracite: slow-burning, less wasteful and polluting forms of coal, required by the Clean Air Act of 1956 for use in smoke control areas.

Substantial cast-concrete fireplaces, faced with mottled beige tiles continued to be popular. A newer shape was shallow, wide and low, with a flat face filled with plain or patterned tiles. As the decade wore on, some fireplaces grew wider, with the mantelpiece forming a shelf across the full width of the chimneybreast and even across the adjacent alcove. Such fireplaces would often be faced with stone crazy paving.

But open fires were not ideal for areas that were used only for short periods, such as bedrooms. Here people tended to use electricity, gas or paraffin. Rising incomes during the 1950s allowed more people to afford more heat and the ownership of electric fires doubled between 1954 and 1960.

Few people had central heating - only five per cent of households by 1960 – and that was usually only two or three radiators and a heated towel rail. No particular form of central heating had yet become dominant and there were a number of systems available: under-floor heating, warm air blowers, ducts, and boilers and radiators.

Many people heated their water by a solid-fuel boiler in the kitchen or a back boiler in the living room fire. An alternative was the Ascot gas or Sadia electric instantaneous water heater, which heated water only as it was used rather than storing it in a tank.

ILLUSTRATION 2
Daily Mail Ideal Home Book, 1957

ILLUSTRATION 1
Personal photograph 1958, image copyright MoDA

ILLUSTRATION 1 This fireplace in a new house in Enfield has the shallow, rectangular shape and flat-tiled face that characterised the modern hearth. In this case the tiles were black; the harmonising wallpaper was red, black and grey.

ILLUSTRATION 2 This type of fireplace was less consciously modern but remained extremely popular throughout the decade.

ILLUSTRATION 3
Catalogue for Woolliscroft fireplaces, about 1960, courtesy of Original Style

ILLUSTRATION 3 These natural stone 'feature' fireplaces, often with an off-centre grate, were fashionable in the late 1950s and 1960s. A similar effect could be seen on the exterior of some new houses of the time when a stone-faced chimneystack would run down the side of a brick house.

ILLUSTRATION 4 Closed stoves were much more efficient, using less fuel and giving out more heat. Some also had thermostatic controls. Glass doors meant that the fire was visible for the comfort factor.

ILLUSTRATION 4
Homes and Gardens, October 1958, courtesy of ESSE

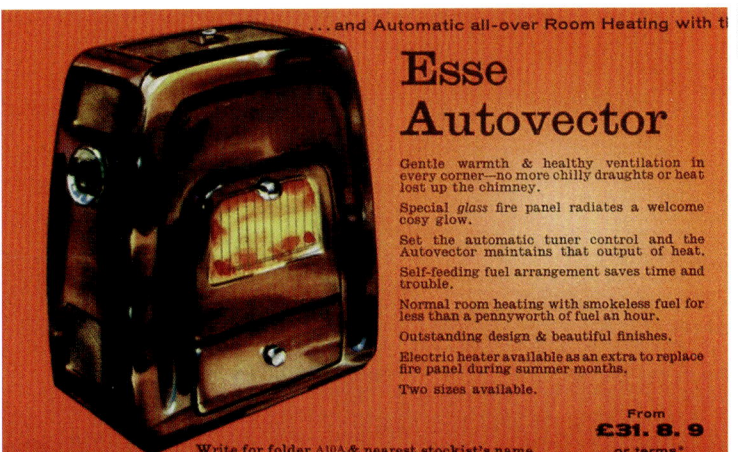

ILLUSTRATION 5
Solid Fuel Housecraft, Elspet Fraser-Stephen, 1950

ILLUSTRATION 6
Houses into Flats: key to conversion,
Charles Woodward and others, 1947

ILLUSTRATION 5 A boiler in the kitchen provided the family's hot water and perhaps fed a couple of radiators and a heated towel rail. Although gas and oil was available, solid fuel was by far the most usual. Boilers were now available with thermostats and easy clean surfaces but it was still a lot of work to carry the fuel, tend the fire, clear the ashes and clean up all the dust and soot.

ILLUSTRATION 6 The instantaneous gas water heater worked by passing cold water over a gas flame. This had the advantage of heating only the water that was actually used. One such heater in the bathroom could provide the water for both the bath and the basin. Another one would be needed in the kitchen.

ILLUSTRATION 7 There were three radiators and a fireplace for supplementary warmth in this large living room in an architect-designed house in Buckinghamshire. Such comprehensive heating provision was quite unusual at this date.

ILLUSTRATION 7
Ideal Home, May 1955, photographer: Stanley Chapman,
© *www.timeincukcontent.com*

ILLUSTRATION 8
Daily Mail Ideal Home Book, 1957

ILLUSTRATION 8 In these early days of central heating, there were a variety of systems on offer and radiators had not yet emerged as the most popular form. In the warm-air method, air passed through a hidden heating unit and circulated around the house through ducts, entering the rooms through grilles in the wall. There is a grille just behind the little girl in this advertisement.

BATHROOMS

In 1951, thirty-seven per cent of all households, mainly those in the older, rented sector, were without a fixed bath. But all new homes had a bathroom, even though space restrictions meant that it was generally quite small and had to incorporate the WC. Larger homes sometimes also had a ground floor cloakroom with a WC and hand basin, but it was most unusual for there to be more than one bathroom.

Fixtures and fittings were designed for easy cleaning, with smoothly rounded edges. For obvious reasons, finishes were usually waterproof. Walls were tiled or gloss- or enamel-painted. Lino, rubber and plastic were serviceable floor coverings.

The bath, with fitted side panels, was usually placed in the corner of the room. Most wash basins were free-standing, either on chrome legs or with the pipes hidden in a ceramic pedestal; but some had a cupboard underneath or, for a more luxurious effect, were built into a unit which incorporated a work surface, shelves and drawers. The cistern for the WC could be either high-level or, for a more up-to-date look, low.

Coloured fittings and paints introduced a decorative element into this essentially utilitarian room. Pastel shades were popular – especially pink, yellow and blue. The curtains were sometimes patterned and there were new plastic fabrics especially for this purpose.

The 1950s bathroom could be quite chilly. Only a small minority of homes had central heating. Some people had a heated towel rail or an electric fire fixed high up on the wall but electric heating was expensive. Although many people had instant water heaters, a good number were reliant on the hard work of a solid fuel boiler. All of this made bathing something of an unpleasant chore, especially in winter. For many families bath-night came only once a week.

ILLUSTRATION 1
The Happy Home, the Gas Council, about 1950

ILLUSTRATION 2
Glass in Your Home, The Glass Advisory Council, 1950s, courtesy of NSG Group

ILLUSTRATION 1 This is a well-equipped but not luxurious bathroom, with an Ascot heater to provide instant hot water. Pale pink was a popular choice, seen here in the tiles, wash basin and plastic curtains.

ILLUSTRATION 2 The white bathroom suite, with its pedestal basin, low-level cistern and chrome fittings, is set off against pale yellow and grey, shiny wall tiles.

ILLUSTRATION 3 This built-in unit was advertised as useful, easy to clean and attractive. The advertisement presents a more decorated and luxurious bathroom than was common at the time.

ILLUSTRATION 4 With limited heating, and before the days of tumble dryers, it was difficult to dry washing and wet towels. The home-made electric-powered drying box on the left is an up-dated version of a clothes horse. It is shown painted to match the bath, basin and bathroom cabinet.

ILLUSTRATION 3
Homes and Gardens, June 1959, courtesy of Formica Group

ILLUSTRATION 4
Practical Householder, January 1957, © www.timeincukcontent.com

BATHROOMS 61

FURTHER READING

Conekin, B., (2003), *'The autobiography of a nation'. The 1951 Festival of Britain,* Manchester University Press, Manchester

Gray, C., (2014), *Fifties house,* Conran Octopus, London

Hoskins, L., (1998) *Living rooms: 20th-century interiors at the Geffrye Museum,* Geffrye Museum, London

Jackson, L., (1994), *'Contemporary': architecture and interiors of the 1950s,* Phaidon, London

Jackson, L., (1991), *The new look: design in the fifties,* Thames and Hudson, London

Quinn, B., (2004), *Mid-century modern: interiors, furniture, design details,* Conran Octopus, London

Ravetz, A. and Turkington, R., (2011), *The place of home: English domestic environments, 1914-2000,* Routledge, London

Ryan, D., (1997), *The ideal home through the 20th century,* Hazar, London

Turner, M., et al, (1989), *A popular art: British wallpapers 1930-1960,* Middlesex Polytechnic, London

Walker, S., (2012), *1950s modern: British style and design,* Shire, Oxford